Bookshelves of the mind
by
S2C Writers at Space2Create

Dedicated to Dave Stretch 1943 -2021

"All that's needed is time passing.
Endurance, love, will make it so."   Dave Stretch

S2C Writers are

Adrian

Alex

Alexandra (Lexie) Harrison

Claire Griffel

Dave Stretch

Debbie Nicholas

Katie

Malcolm Nicholas

Mat Butler

Natasha k - w

Phil Williams

Debbie was born and brought up in Greater London,
where her mum still lives in the same house that Debbie entered
62 years ago, aged 6 weeks.

Her first five poems are about her parents, particularly her dad.

Debbie moved to Kendal in 2007 and felt like she was permanently on holiday – surrounded by fells and with the river and castle nearby.

She says that feeling has never gone away.

Shoes Like These

Brown shoes, shining from regular polishing, leather uppers and soles, sourced from a special shop in Holborn to suit a high instep.

Shoes like these had travelled to Burma in the 2nd World War and walked across the country driving out the Japanese.

Shoes like these had come home and had to adjust to civvy street with three jobs to pay the mortgage and six mouths to feed.

Shoes like these had run a scout group and taken the family camping all over the UK.

Shoes like these had been made redundant and been found making wine at seven in the morning.

Shoes like these had gradually adjusted to being retired and had embraced life until, at the age of 90,

Shoes like these had been struck down by a stroke and the ensuing dementia.

Shoes like these are helped into a wheelchair or step slowly, unsteadily, from room to room.

But shoes like these are happy in their own way, they still live in that same home looked after by a loving wife.

Shoes like these will be 100 in January and still they walk on.

June 2019

Everyday Hero

Mum is an everyday hero, who cares for dad
as he travels backwards to his earliest self.
She spoons blended food into his baby-bird mouth
and holds a straw to his clamped-closed lips.

Mum coaxes dad's reluctant legs
into standing unsteadily, leading him as he walks.
They travel together on their uncertain journey
into the blind landscape of dementia.

2017

Silence

Silent as the womb, dad sits

So few words pass his lips

Silent as a tomb, dad sits

No more jokes, no more quips

What is in his mind?

What pictures does he see?

A winter seaside town

Is no quieter than he

With the passing of each day

He has so little speech

Locked silently away

His thoughts are out of reach

2018

Happy Place

Dad has changed again
He has moved into a happier self
His long ago laugh has returned
Reminding me of earlier times

He sings old football chants
And wartime marching songs
And counts his legs
'one, two, that's right'

I don't have my old dad back
But today, I have glimpses of him

2019

Skin

His skin is paper thin with age

The veins like the contours of his life

Mapping out his journey across continents

For our second hand memories

The tell-tale sign of a Burmese sun

Patterns the delicate skin on his head

The soldier he was is still evident

In the way he sits, the songs he sings

But now he is the cared-for

And that same skin is cleansed by another,

Has moisturiser rubbed in each day

Until it is as soft as a baby's

As his life unwinds back from 100

July 2019

The Kiss

Mum bent over dad
And kissed him
On the head
And the tip of his nose
As she did every night
Before he went to sleep

Only this time, it was morning
And he would sleep forever
In memory of Jack Hull (1920 – 2020)

Empty Chair

No dad sat in brown armchair
The space in the room is still young
An empty place, he is not there
No words or songs half-sung

I mourn the loss but not his passing
It was his time, he was ready to leave
No life is forever, nothing everlasting.
But we'll meet again, I do believe

I miss you dad, and will forever
Miss your care and common sense
You worked so hard, were funny and clever
Memories now are my recompense

Jan 2021

The Ending of the Day

The colours in the sky fade to grey
As I watch the ending of the day
Peach and orange are replaced by black
The sun has set there is no turning back

Look again, no colour left behind
The blue has faded, nothing to remind
Of the sky once so full of sun
Now a life that is nearly gone

Recovery of the Light

The mist hovers above the field
Like gossamer in the light
We wend our way slowly home
And watch the death of night

The M6 is quiet and still
The cat's-eyes lead the way
It is early in the morning
Before the start of day

Sun meanders through the clouds
Lighting up the mist
Which hangs like a spiders web
That's been rain kissed

Memories

I leaf through my memories
Both sad and sweet
There is balm for my soul
But the photographs only tell
Half the story

The shutter falls with a click
And captures one moment
But many either side are lost
Except to my memory

I remember the leaves that
Have fallen and are lost
Except for those I choose
To hold dear in my heart

Or not so dear,
Only emerging
From the cracks
In the night

Glimmer
A glimmer of light, shone through the heavy clouds, lightening the day.
A glimmer of hope, entered her heart through the darkness, lifting her spirits.
A glimmer of an idea, started to take shape through the fog, sparking her interest.
Sometimes a glimmer is all you need to turn things around.

A Hole To Let The Light In

Hollowed out heart
To let the love in
Hole in the sky
To let the light in
Hole in the soul
Fit to frighten
Soul full of love
Sure to enlighten

Time Passes
Spring passes and I remember the soft green days of youth
Summer passes and I remember the rose blush of womanhood
Autumn passes and I remember the wrinkled russet of old age
Winter passes and I remember nothing

Hidden Gem

They said she was a hidden gem
Sparkling in the light
They said all manner of lovely things
That she was oh so bright

But she could not accept their truths
And so she just took flight
Up into the air she flew
And soon was out of sight

Why is it harder to accept
A compliment than a slight?
What makes us shun the world
And put up such a fight?

I'm sure we all have hidden gems
That shine right through the night
The secret is to own them
And just enjoy the light

On the Edge

In the mythical forest the branches weave and wave in unison

and the roots are like a tempestuous sea

There are people warning us of the dangers

of going too close to the edge

But we don't heed them because

we believe we have the invincibility of youth

That if we fell, the underground

waves would catch us gently in a swathe of dreams

We are dizzy with the beauty of the sky

where the blues, reds and yellows blend powerfully

and lead us into a magical world

where the trees form a hammock that rocks us in their embrace

We are safe in their outstretched arms

as we balance on the edge of reason

Malcolm was born and raised in Kendal. He loves to run which is why he can often be seen, wobbly-kneed and gasping for breath, hanging onto bus stops.

When he was a teenager his grandpa told him that he was distantly related to William Shakespeare. Malcolm spent the next 50 years trying to emulate the Bard, moving from tragedy to farce, before deciding to be himself.

Malcolm returned to Kendal to live in 2007. After over 25 years in the Probation Service in Nottingham and South East London and 10 years as a Carer Support Worker in Kendal he gave up paid work in 2017.

Since then he has had more time to concentrate on drinking tea and daydreaming. He got married to the wonderful Debbie in 2021. Luckily she also drinks a lot of tea and has lots of dreams.

Coming up for Air

I strode across the fields
Over the gates, through the stiles
I walked for miles.
I sought the greenest valleys
Explored the distant dales
I counted all the fell tops that I reached
I ran through every grain of sand
On every beach, in every land.
I climbed the tallest mountain
And felt the cool peace freshening my lungs
I realised that I'd come up for air by being there.
My silent breath smelled clean and purified
I loved myself as much as anyone.
I felt the sunrise
I heard the stars as they surveyed
The space between eternities.
They told each other jokes about humanity
And showed me how to reach the
Pinnacle
Where enlightenment rules our days.
At night I still come down
Floating past the moon
To remind myself of everything
I've lost and gained.
I came up here for air
And then I stayed.

Flowers for Martin

Snowdrops keep falling from my eyes
Tiny roots that find their way
To be trapped by the earth
As much as they are free

Bluebells will soon be ringing
For Martin and his song
Chiming more than singing
Searching for a long time
Hoping they're not wrong
To breeze away with
Pretty tunes and words

We gasp in disbelief
At what's occurred
Within their flowery bed
The crocuses are dead
The daffs all shrivelled

Their shadows spread across
A field of tears

In Memory of
Martin Clark 1953 - 2021

Dancing in the Empty Spaces

If life is a ballet

If life is a jig

If the steps that we take are

The steps in a waltz

If we're all at the ceilidh

Or shaking our hips

Twisting and turning

And leaping so high

Finding the room on the dancefloor

To jive

Seeing the pleasure

The smiles on the faces

From dancing

In those empty spaces

Finding the Kindness

Finding the world where kindness
Splashes around your feet
Like the incoming tide

Finding the city where kindness
And pity can make us all smile
As we're touching
The hands of the homeless

Finding the town where kindness
Abounds, and strangers will save us
From danger

Finding the street
Where we'll never meet oppression
And unkindly words.

Finding the kindness that's hidden
Among all the flotsam and jetsam
Of a seaweed shore.

Wind

Cold and golden, the wind shatters

Powdering dust in

The breath of the breeze

Her ashes

Frozen in silence

Rag

My mother was doing that thing she did. That thing with the rag in the sink. When she looked as though she was holding it under the cold water tap. As she turned away from the sink she lifted her right arm up and back. The thing is this – right. Are you guessing yet? Sometimes she threw it at dad. Sometimes she threw it at me. Sometimes she never threw it at all. Sometimes it was soaking wet. Other times it was just a dry rag. She said she did that thing to get our attention when we were ignoring her. She said the uncertainty of it all was better at making us think about what we were doing or not doing. The cold damp patch the rag sometimes left on my shirt was really annoying. I mean really, really annoying. One time I threw the rag back at her.

I couldn't stop thinking about the rag when we buried her.

The Seeker

Was it the depths of her soul you sought?

Was it the flashing gold you could not catch,

The flowers anchored to the water's edge

Her Celtic beauty as she picked the berries from the bushes

Her flowing gown coloured with a rainbow

The basket which she rests upon a stone

Filled with forest fruits and stolen sunshine

Her sometimes smiling glimpses through dark trees

Her playful eyes, majestic in their power

Yet hinting at her vulnerability

Do you seek her or mere perfection?

Rumi

Because I could not sleep
I rose from my warm bed and crept into the kitchen
Closing the door as quietly as I could.

I caught my foot on the dining table
As I tried to find the light switch
And swore under my breath.

I heated water in the kettle
Poured it on the tea bag carefully
Then waited for it to cool.
I sipped it slowly
Savouring the taste of chamomile

Because I could not sleep
I sat and thought
About the things I'd lost
Or never sought.

The Winter 10K

Cold enough to freeze a flood
Feet engulfed in seas of mud
Double-knotted soggy laces
Tie me to the run's embraces

Chilled feet freeze
In floods of cold and mud
The run holds me
Tight as the laces
Hold my shoes

Swimming

You are a swimmer
And racism is the waves

Gone are the dispossessed
Turning in their graves
Seeking justice not revenge
For all those who were slaves

Whose dreams were drowned
Whose hopes washed away
Whose blood is our freedom
Whose humanity saves us

Whose laughter surprises
As the tide turns away

You are a swimmer
And the tide turns today

Black Lives Matter

Truth

One day I met the truth riding through dark forests

In search of knowledge

to impart to those in search of truth.

I asked if it was true that all people can be liars.

She nodded sadly

then carried on her journey

searching for a better truth to tell.

The Lipstick Remains

Do you yearn for a time when gas bills were paid
When a loaf of sliced bread did not break the bank
When Ukraine didn't know the meaning of 'tank'
When hope reigned eternal and fear just sank
To the bottom of the sea, the depths of despair.

Do you miss those sweet years
 When everyone laughed at the jokes that you told
When Burnley were champions year after year
When youngsters played nicely
You ruffled their hair and they called you sir

The world before lifeache, did it really exist
Or did we invent it when were pissed?
But the lipstick remains
So I know I was kissed
By your trembling lips
And loved
To the soul

Soul Music

I sensed the shadow disappear as rainclouds thundered overhead
I heard the open window bang and felt the splintered glass
I saw the spots of blood soak into sodden carpet, destroying any
comfort with pain and cold and fear.

I reached under the bed searching for the blackened crystal box
And inside that my hopes, my very essence.
I'd kept my spirit like this, out of danger, protecting it from floods,
from pestilence
Now my soul was stolen.

But that was many songs ago.
We celebrated long into the night
When music found my soul dancing and laughing
The thieves all vanquished.
Returned, reborn, we'd won the bloody fight
For my own soul was only ever mine.

Pet Rock Day: September 5th 2021

I took my pet rock Sally for a walk along the coast
Because it was her birthday
And she likes this walk the most

We watched the waves all crashing against the harbour wall
When I told her to be careful
She didn't mind at all

Sally used to be a pebble before I took her home
She caught my eye one Sunday
I raised her as my own

Ignoring sand and gravel Sally grew to be a rock
Her friends were all so proud of her
Though it wasn't a big shock

She went on to be famous when she joined the Rolling Stones
The riffs she played were legendary
She held the stage alone

But she always likes to be back home when it comes to Pet Rock Day
She finds the waves that gave her life
And gives thanks to the spray
In Beadnell Bay.

My name is Phil and I was born in Kendal and brought up in the Kentmere Valley in the Lake District.
I wandered the hills, cycling them and running them.

I write from the heart and soul and mind - my work filled with tears and joys, life as I see - it very much from my own perspective.
Some writing full of pain anguish and torments other of nature and some humorous, some very dark, some bright, some I am told powerful!

Phil Williams

Treasures of Delight!

Treasures upon the bookshelves of the mind where the shelves are lined
with books full of memories of your past each page telling its own story
of your life.

Some happy some sad full of joys full of woes all of those prose and
poetry of your existence.

Stories of all your traumas retold over and over your memories each so
hard to hear each page bending your ear, from year to year your life
unfolds unravelling the past many books in thoughts
as yet untold!

Ready to be told!

Phil Williams

All today's yesterdays

Yesterday is today is today inside out,

Tomorrow is today forgotten about,

Yesterday is today forgotten about,

Tomorrow is today inside out!

Phil Williams

Love actually is!

Love actually is just more than just a word,

Love actually is unconditional,

Love actually is never giving up on someone,

Love actually is giving not to receive,

Love actually is true and oh so wonderful a feeling to have,

Love actually is emotions — thoughts and feelings — all of those little gestures

which mean so very much to the one you love so much.

Love actually is gazing into one another's eyes and getting lost in the moment,

Spending hours admiring your lover.

Love actually is more than just a word,

But so much more to have and to hold

With gold in your heart and purity of soul.

Love actually does make the world revolve.

Love actually is.

Phil Williams

Cogs Turning

Cogs turning

mind whirring

cogs turning

FLASHBACKS occurring

mind working overtime

brain churning traumas

recurring mind in a turmoil

traumatised beyond normal parameters.

Thoughts undeserving

brain barely maintaining -

functions all askew

nightmares taking their turn

dreams tortured -

waking from nightmares

hyperventilating-

not knowing how to cope -

way out of my scope!

Night time thinking -

night time thoughts distorted

from highs to extreme lows

depression all encompassing

thoughts, plans, wishes overwhelming -

life not worth existing, life past caring

why bother continuing, life's too much

not enough proper thinking all disjointed

sometimes wish I was still drinking.

Oblivion seems so welcoming

obliteration of all of this thinking

no more - no more - no more.

Ending pain - finishing

not living barely functioning

not

really

doing

any

more

than

sinking!

Phil Williams

My Psychiatrist

I think my Psychiatrist is shite

Talentless careless and Cold

So she'll get a promotion alright!

I'd like to challenge her to a fight if ever I were so bold

I think they broke the bloody mould

I think my Psychiatrist is shite so she'll get a promotion alright!

Would you say my Psychiatrist's a witch?

I think she is starting to itch

Or is it she is starting to twitch?

No, I think it's just she's a bitch!

I think my Psychiatrist is shite so she'll get a promotion alright!!

She never gets anything right

All the drugs she hands out either give me bad vibes or keep me awake half the night

My Psychiatrist isn't so bright she hands out pills at random it's not as if I "demand 'em"

I think my Psychiatrist is shite which doesn't give me much delight

She never did get that promotion and it really gives me such emotion.

So suffice it to say, I get the last say at the end of the day

And it's finally the end of an ill chosen career!

Phil Williams

Timorous wee beastie

The n'ere to do and timorous wee beastie roams the moors of bonny wee Scotland, the wee beastie scuttles and hides amongst the thistles and tussocks is a devils own job to catch one or track it despite it having five legs and to catch or trap one is a real task. Better known as the haggis but if ere you should catch one beware you don't take hold of it by its fifth leg for although ye will not cause it a fright you are more likely to bring it delight but beware if ye do catch one of these wee laddies then beware the bite for it is deadly and is sure to cause your demise. Never underestimate this fellow of the moors for he can evade ye and be as hard to catch as the wind they are clever if not to say wiley and fond of staying out of sight but should ye be lucky enough, to catch this rare delicacy it tastes divine and is a feast upon which to dine.

A poem by Philip Williams with a contribution by Anni!

Silver Birch

I am soft in my strength

I yield to the mind. I bend to the ice.

I move with energy of "what is."

I am the face of the feminine.

Let me show you how to be flexible

in the face of challenge.

Let me show you how to dance the dance of life.

Let me impregnate you with the seed of possibility in each

new moment.

Let me show you how to tap into and fulfil

the blueprint of your life.

Phil Williams September 2019

TORN

Torn from your fractured thoughts from your plagued mind your pitiful existence torn into a thousand tiny fragments your mind - mind fragmented your memories twisted dishevelled and putrid!

Why is my fractured life so disjointed and distraught? I know not the answer but am left to ponder yonder what it is all about. Life can throw so many a mountain to climb both hazardous and treacherous.

Life is a great battle each and every moment of every day.

Each and every moment torn apart and twisted - turned upside down inside out!

Topsy turvy wish life was not so squirmy.

Life is going to beyond hell and back and forth so many times I forgot myself, your very essence your sense of self worth and your sense of who you were or are now?!

Phil Williams

For You

You are an amazing and brilliant comet which blazes a trail across the night sky.

Outshining all it passes, on its way.

You travel life's journey touching many hearts and bring much light into each and every life.

Every life you touch you bring so much joy and oh so much happiness. Mine is but one of many.

How I do love you my beloved, you have touched my heart in a way that I have not yet experienced.

You brought me happiness the like of which I have not known and such serenity.

This was all a long time coming in my life.

Now it has arrived I must and will hold onto it forever, for life is but short lived.

We must enjoy and make the most of every sweet and tender moment.

If I have brought you a glimpse of what is possible between us, then I will remain as happy as I am right now.

You have fulfilled my dreams.

I can only say what is in my heart and in my mind and both are crying out

Yes at last I have met my one true love!

I love you.

Phil Williams

Catacombs

Deep within the dark realms of the mind's inner sanctums there lie dark tunnels dark corners and dark cavernous spaces the catacombs of the dark recesses of the brain where lurk dark shadows and evil demons waiting their chance to pounce and destroy tour every fibre of being drag you deeper into a pit of despair —

doom and gloom. Catacombs torment your very soul break your spirit take you deeper into the labyrinth of the mind.

The deeper you go the gloomier your spirit becomes these demons and spirits of your past existence haunt your waking and sleeping moments and when you least expect it you will be led deeper inside the mind where the most frightening elements of the psyche lie!

If you believe you have sunk to the deepest darkest most depressing and scary place you have ever been taken then think again! For the mind holds far more sinister feelings thoughts and places to be dragged down to!

Phil Williams

Friendship

Friends have come and gone in my life
Sometimes quickly
Sometimes lingering
But I will always remember them
For friends may come and friends may go
But the special ones will always remain
Safe to cry and safe to share
No matter how long it has been
We know each other's quirks and fears
We smile and laugh as Summer nears
Our friends remain some new some old
Some are silver
Some are gold.

Phil Williams

Mat Butler was born in Sheffield and after many years meandering through careers, degrees and accidental occupations settled up running an arts charity and being creative a lot. A painter by preference Mat uses his writing to reflect on memories, mental health and the consequences of type 1 diabetes from childhood.

"These poems I dedicate to my lovely wife Wendy in her daily struggle with Vascular Dementia, without whom I would have died many times over."

Still

Still I wait,

Wondering at celestial grace,

For the world to turn in a unified direction..

Still I wonder why,

We look beyond the meanders,

And only see the river diverge.

Still I only hear,

The rattling of swords

Like wooden toys,

Wielded with little boy bravado.

Still I find no clarity,

A world of one mind,

With a meaningful purpose.

Still I despair,

Over descending futures,

With no prospect of change.

Still I see division.

So still I wait.

Still.

Mat Butler 2021

A Stroll With Death

I remember once I walked a while with Death in my shadow,

He kept pace with me in his long sinuous stride,

Silent for a time.

Then in language just beyond my perception he conversed,

With the voices in my head,

That silent watcher, my evil eye, that directs malevolent thought,

To bias my negative persuasions.

Then his thoughts turned to my own and he spoke directly to me,

"Do you wish now to come with me?"

Was his offer at that time.

The words of my reply I chose with care:

"I am not quite ready to decide, a few more steps if you please,

And an answer I will give."

As I spoke he moved from my shadow to my side,

I felt his hand upon my shoulder.

I must confess I almost accepted his offer,

For dark thoughts were ever my companion.

Then a distant creative desire lost deep within my soul,

Rose up and protested my doom.

"My apologies Sir, but now is not my time. Some other day I may accept,

And take me then you must."

With palpable disappointment He was gone.

A burden lifted from my mind.

A close escape but decision made,

I strode upon my road alone.

Mat Butler 2017

Virtually

It seemed a visceral reality,

Neurones fired as skin skimmed cold metal,

The rustle of the western breeze,

Dragged tired hairs awake,

And sonorous vibration rattled inner ear.

Fear rose with distant waves,

As the cliffs pondered lofty ambitions,

Seabirds called coded warnings,

As I stepped tentatively towards the edge.

Finally I plunged into pixelated oblivion,

As realities floor claimed me.

Mat Butler 2020

There You Are

There you were.

A perception in the corner of my eye,

Effervescent in those red shoes.

You stamp your feet,

And the world thunders,

You click your heels,

And dimensions fracture.

You challenged the Gods,

And were lost to my sight.

Really, you are just a dancer.

Effervescent in those red shoes,

A perception in the corner of my eye,

There you are.

Mat Butler 2021

Stationary

In circumstantial custodial existence,

An experience sharpened by ineffectuality,

And laboured with exceptional disturbed grace.

Dutybound to care by internal loyalties,

Yet bereft and adrift,

In an emotional ocean.

Searching the horizon for that island of madness,

Where once certain futures,

Play out like passionless horror.

A grim necklacing by harsh realities,

Where one receives the concrete overcoat,

Of this new life.

Mat Butler 2021

1980

On a hot summer's day,

My meandering thoughts,

Travel to the fake brown leather,

Of the rear seats in a dark green Volvo 240.

Cigarette smoke and stale beer,

Two families confined within,

My hot bare legs trade blows,

With the annoying daughter.

The radio flails loudly,

With Wimbledon cheers,

And sardonic commentary.

The thwack of ball on racket,

And my detached observing spirit,

Shares the sentiment that resonates,

Through the humid air from crackle speakers,

"You cannot be serious!"

Mat Butler 2021

Silence

In a world of all consuming communication,

Where the omnipotent ping chases attention,

A whimpering child.

Problems hunt us in salivating packs,

And flocks of vulturous words,

Circle poised to spew onto screens.

Music is distracting confusions,

While life vacillates loudly.

Then I sit alone,

Disconnected for ignorance,

Taking refuge,

In silence.........

Mat Butler 2021

Flutter Bye

I observe their progress,

Lives distinct by beauty alone,

Eyes drawn like moths,

But the expression contempts.

Darting and flapping movements confuse,

Predators left biting air.

Exceptionally reacting,

That flutter stings,

With a pointing barb of sharp words.

They pause,

A brief retail opportunity,

Sucking up frivolous nectar,

With points tripling in anticipation.

On to the next.

They preen at refreshment,

Those claws working to glam,

And then gone,

That moment passed across my vision,

Attracting opto-motor reflexes,

Time and again.

Differing colours and flavours,

So many,

Fluttering by.

Mat Butler 2021

Meandering Thoughts

Like oceans they ebb and flow,

Eddies and currents swirl,

Crash in waves that build and fade.

Colours painted over a canvas,

Dragged and formed with a

Brush of experience.

Looking to the heavens,

Wisps merge and collide woolly and white,

Holding brief forms to evaporate.

Suddenly invigorated,

They leap and explode,

Furiously expanding with power and energy.

Until a pen is required,

And they hold substance,

Desperately scratched in inky abandon.

Mat Butler 2021

Katie's grandma was a self proclaimed wordsmith
and wrote prolifically throughout Katie's life.
This ignited Katie's passion for words and the craft of writing.

She hopes to mirror some of her grandma's lessons
over the years.

Into the wilderness

Lights spread across the inky sky
Incandescent green dancers overhead
Fill the night sky with an eerie glow
The snow lies crisp on the ground.

He pads on, crunching underfoot
His coat a marbled grey
His body strong and warm
Panting to the sound of his brethren's howls.

The scent of pine lingers
That woody smell that nips at your nostrils
The pine needles creak, a carpet
Rustles come from the undergrowth

The wind is the only sound now
A wind mirroring the howls of before
The landscape is bleak
Bleak but beautiful
The silence, the stillness, a bated breath
This is the wilderness

Serendipity

We roll the dice in life
It seems there is no control of those little numbers that fall into
place
Life is a game, are we mere pawns within it

We can weight those dice, roll the wrist as we throw
Paths are open to us
It may seem one path is the way we must go
But the choice is there, we can follow the one less trodden

Destiny is a dark cloud
It hangs heavy on weakened hearts.
The inevitability of life can stifle our steps
We must see the sun and dance through the rain
Make the cloud our own and get wet.

The passage of time

How quick, yet how slow

Time is so easily distorted

When we are children a year seems a lifetime

Yet childhood goes so fast

At whose hand does the hourglass drain of sand?

Mess

My mind is a mess

A chaotic den

A rat's nest full of ideas and questions

A lot of rubbish there too!

Where I left that thing from 5 years ago

My mind is a mess

Sometimes I fall over in it

Consumed by the mounting accumulation of stuff

I need a hoover.

Capture

I have a net made of loose rope
It lives deep inside
I use it to capture moments
Blinks of the eye
All so easily passing us by

My net sweeps and scoops up memories
Supplanting them deep in my grey matter
Watching the little ones grow
Remembering the laughs giggles, tickles and shouts
Those happy butterflies caught in my net

But sometimes things get stuck
Dark memories stick like glue to my net
Soon blocking out all light
The butterflies cannot enter
They cannot fly

How do I free my net of this tar like ooze?
Let the net breathe and sweep freely again?
Catching more of the light and less of the thick molasses

I must clean my thoughts
Sleep away the sticky residue
Awaken with a new vessel ready to scoop up the smiles again.

Today

The snow falls softly

Silvery flakes slip onto soft soil

The dark mud rejuvenated by this fresh white carpet

The landscape is reimagined

Icicles hang like stars from bridges and trees.

The word renewed, reborn and clean

Bright and calm, sparkling flickers in the winter sun

In the tree sits a robin redbreast

Proud in his resplendent plumage

I watch him slowly pick the seeds from in between patches of

snowy ground

Carefully choosing the brightest berries, sweet and plump.

I look out on this new scene

I rejoice to see the coming of winter

The feeling of being born anew

The chill that nips feels refreshing

My energy replenished with a blank slate

I look forward to my recovery.

Exterior/Interior

The exterior looks so calm

A babbling brook over cold land

Barely perceivable movement

The exterior is strong and solid

Unbreakable, unweathered

A smile hides the catacombs below.

But they do feel anger

Inside, buried in an abyss

The interior is hot

It bubbles and burns

Lava trickles from every crack

Choking smoke in the air

The anger lies beneath ready to erupt.

They say don't get angry - the exterior echoes it the interior betrays it.

Ask a leaf

Ask a leaf how they feel

You will get a rich story

What does it feel like to grow from seed?

Slowly stretch, watching the years

Growing wise. Part of an entity

How does it feel in the height if summer?

Warm sun caressing your skin

How does it feel to fall?

To sink down away from your skin, with the knowledge of

the son you will bring.

Lift

Lift me up into the sky

Let me tumble in the zephyr

Dance on the sweet breeze

Fly amongst the clouds.

Lift my heart and soul to be free

Free from the chains of this earthly form.

Silence

The air was palpable

Bated breath hung softly in the city streets

The alien metropolis with no sound

The hustle and bustle quietened

It felt eerie

Seeing the streets empty

On the precipice of impending doom

A single owl broke the silence

One lowly cry before the destruction of a new day

The KINGFISHER

The whispered voices as we looked through the trees

There sat a little hole 3cm across

Found by my dad just the day before

Deep in the mud it sat, easily passed by

The children stood on tiptoes waiting

Holding in the bubbles of excitement

A sudden flash so quick up the river

A fleeting glimpse of incandescent turquoise

The burnt orange underneath

A mere streak of colour in the bleakness

The king of the river returned

I hear a slight squeal behind me

Before hands are clasped back over mouths

Our first kingfisher nest

Mes

There are several different mes
Faces that swap and change
Shape shifting identities

There is the happy me
The mask of contentment that I hold passively to my face
The smile plastered on

Sometimes the mask slips and I transform
Become the other me
A me filled with melancholy and a little darkness
The me who doesn't sleep and can't keep up that smile

But I am more than binary

There is the me that cares
That loves and sees beauty in little things
The me that acts professionally
Watching words like a captain over their platoon

There is the child me, the innocent carefree girl
Who skips through life, unaware of her innate fragility

The angry me, this one I hide
Like a beast in a dungeon
Locked deep away for fear it will destroy the other mes I have created
The many masks I wear.

To end, I would like to share a piece written by my grandma.

The Gift

I watched you smile

With clear and simple grace

I watched you smile

Without a trace of guilt

The memory of your face

Lives in a special place

I watched you smile

Dorothy Walker

Alexandra (Lexie) Harrison was born in Bedfordshire but largely raised in London. Lexie is especially proud of her Cumbrian and Scottish heritage. In 2019 Lexie moved up North, living initially in Lancaster.

Lexie now lives in Kendal, not far from Ulverston where her Father was born.

One of the things that matters most to Lexie is climate change and the impact it has on the future of planet Earth and its inhabitants. She believes we must look after our environment to ensure a brighter future for all those we leave behind.

Enough

Enough Enough Enough

I have had enough

Enough of Striving

Enough of trying to be good enough

There is power in this – freedom

When you surrender space is created

Space to evolve and develop

Space to be authentic

I am enough

We are enough

Lexie Harrison

And the moon said to me...

Cherish the Earth

Cherish your home

Care take the ground, air and sky

Please stay away from here, far away

Love each other and express it

Mother Earth will thank you

Mother Earth will show you

Mother Earth will show you...

Lexie Harrison

Red shoes

She had music in her step!

Her red tap shoes brought delight

Her footprints left notes

Her dress was magical like her steps

The wind moved her, she moved us

Musical trails like paint strokes

Lexie Harrison

This poem was inspired by
a print created by artist Jackie Gaskell

Mountains

I have a history of kitchens without views
Now I look out from my kitchen
onto picturesque mountains
I open my window a little to let the fresh air
in
I'm feeling the freedom this landscape offers
Need to step outside
Barefoot I step onto the grass and breathe in.
The landscape is now a part of me
and I a part of it.

Lexie Harrison

I wanted to include the following quotes
which are important to me

"Discouragement is a negative emotion with more
than one trick up its dark sleeve. It tricks you into
mentally or emotionally dwelling in the very place you
want to leave. Drop all such sorrow permanently by
daring to see through this deception of the
unconscious mind. You have a destination far beyond
where you find yourself standing today"
Guy Finley

"Values are critical guides for making decisions.
When in doubt, they cut through the fog like a beacon
in the night."
Robert Townsend

"Live your beliefs and you can turn the world around."
Henry David Thoreau

I am sharing this poem as it reflects my own
journey through darkness and light

The Weaver

My life is but a weaving
Between my Lord and me
I cannot choose the colours
He worketh steadily

Oft-times He weaveth sorrow
And I, in foolish pride
Forget He sees the upper And I the under side

Not til the loom is silent
And the shuttles cease to fly
Does God unroll the canvas
And explain the reason why

The dark threads are as needful
In the weaver's skilful hand
As the threads of gold and silver
In the pattern He has planned.

Author uncertain

51 Word Fiction

I gladly learnt quite early that

life is a journey, not a destination

Were my goals my destination?

Which goal would be my final

destination?

Destination is destiny?

Feel the fear and do it anyway I say

When will I arrive?

Does it matter?

I think I'll end with a natter

Lexie Harrison

Adrian was born in Scotland, but grew up in Wisconsin.

From the age of 17 he thought of himself as a Buddhist.

He loves anything that makes the mind calm and peaceful,

like meditation or going for walks.

If he's not meditating or out on a walk,

u can probably find him reading books about Buddhism.

Once upon a time in the North

Once upon a time in the North
Santa was in his workshop
He had no time to stop
The elves were working thru the night
With all their might
They had too much to do
They had no time at least ...
To be blue

R U angry?

R U angry?

R U patient?

R U angry that you have to be patient?

There is no virtue greater than patience,

and no evil greater than anger.

The sound of silence

What is the sound of silence?

What is the sound of 1 hand clapping?

Is it better to have some noise in the background?

Or is it more peaceful for there to be silence?

Our thoughts r like inner noise.

Thru meditating there can be inner stillness.

Smile

Smile – something that let's others know u r well,

something that makes others feel good when they

see it,

after a long day,

it's good to see a smile.

Like an Umbrella

Like how an umbrella can shield u from
the rain,
a peaceful positive mind
can shield u
from all problems.
Just like how u need to open an
umbrella for it to work, u need to open
ur mind by making it peaceful and
positive.

Mingle

Let us mingle with others,
To mingle is
To connect
With others.

I like to mingle.

Do not meddle
When u mingle,

Do not mingle
While u meddle.

The seven rules of life

Remember the happiness of others

is just as important as ur own.

Do not hate,

do not judge,

always have something

to look forward to,

avoid junk food,

have a healthy breakfast,

feed ur spirit.

Hear Seed Power

Do u hear the power of an oak tree?

It begins life as a seed.

Then it grows and grows.

It has a silent power,

maybe u can't hear its power but u can

feel it.

The seed of an oak tree needs to be

watered for it to grow,

it takes time and doesn't happen

instantly.

Do u hear the power of an oak tree?

Interior Exterior

Our interior world
in our minds
is very important,
we need to establish peace
in our minds
or our external world
will not be pleasant,
once we have interior peace,
we will have peace
in our exterior world.

Me Myself I

I do not exist inherently. I am impermanent.
I am not my mind.
I am not my body, I am not the collection of my body and mind.
I am not something other than my body and mind because there is nothing else. I am emptiness, my impermanence makes me empty. I am here, now.
But in 100 years I won't be.

May you be still

May u be still enough,

to enjoy nature,

to watch ur thoughts,

to know what u have,

to react without anger,

to be free.

Claire Griffel thinks she's a bit of a funny mixture
of heritage and happenings.

She seems to have had only one motivation in life - seeking out
adventure.

She thanks everyone and everything for that.

Drift

Float with movement of the waves

Relentless waves encouraging waves

Waves to herald all sorts of change

In the journey

Inhabited by memories

The wood of a tree

host to hungry insects

Time passes

Inner circles widen

Roots take hold

For the drifting to finally

cease

Lost

I once was lost

Never expected to return. I once lost people
I called true loves.

I once lost children I thought would be born.

I swear

I will not stop

Until

I have lost

My breath

My lone tree

This tree grows on my horizon
since I moved to a room with a view
it has returned my gaze for years
every time I look out
it appears to me.
This tree beckoned daily
when no-one else came
until one day at dawn I walked
to find this tree to see
what I could see.
This tree grows around a stone wall
impossible to tell where the wall ends
and this tree begins.
Such a relief to have a wall
without fixed limits.
This tree lives apart with grace
offers branches for the birds
a home for cobwebs and their spiders
allows wire and barbs to penetrate
with open generosity.
This tree an ancient oak
brims gleams with endurance.
In mourning I made this visit
alone together in a first embrace
my windows staring back at me.

Door

I opened the door of the Labour in Vain

My local you know

There he was spread over the bar stool

Telling a tale

Supping his Guinness

And wiping the froth from his beard

I was won by his tale

The affair was short lived

Years later I opened the door of the Labour in Vain

He was there back again

And the same tale that he told

Was already too old

For me to fall for it

Once again

I'm not a poppy person

I'm not a poppy person

I wish it never was

I wish I didn't have to know

The horror of what we did

I wish I didn't have to go to memorial stones

And hear the bugle play

I wish the poppies were not red

I wish no skin was torn

I wish no-one was dead

Just because we wanted more

And more and more and more

And now my poppies are all white and I pray

on my knees

for peace every night

Only

They were sole survivors

We admired them

Because they were

They fled

With courage

They denied

With strength

They shared with love

Their eyes

Pools

Windows

Wells

Open

For

Life to shine

And lift

Us here

And there

To

Soulful embrace

Dust

I am an intelligent duster

I don't dust often

But when I dust

I dust extremely carefully

I know where the light falls

And shows the gatherings

Of skin and mites and particles

And it is there where the light falls

That I move the surface coverings

To shine with the illusion

That no dust remains elsewhere

It is extremely satisfying and happens

5 times a year.

what is it to be human

Is it human or huwoman
Is there any in between
and what
do all these personal pronouns really mean ...
I bought a sign for my
partner
it said "Man Cave watch out"
to hang above his door.
Then I thought
let's change it
add two letters
and
have a present
just for me.
W and O make it woman cave.
But when the top popped off my felt tip pen
the letters changed their shape!
I have a humane cavern instead
will that be better for us -
Them as those who remain?

Red

I listened in horror to the news another oil tanker had hit rocks
near the Gulf of Mexico and everyone was horrified at the tonnes
and tonnes of oil that would wash up on beaches that would
coat creatures of the sea land and air.

I cried.

I was waiting for the pictures of sea birds with feathers
heavy and useless coated in the oil we thought we needed.

An expert was called for he was good with oil leaks and holes in tankers.

He stopped the leak and millions of living beings were saved.

His name Red Adare.

For him I say a prayer.

The shelf

She showed promise

They thought she might make it

to the top shelf

Though it was strange ...

each time the top shelf was very obviously

within her grasp

she declined it.

She turned away moved away went away

and found

an entirely different place.

Where's the consistency they cried

why oh why must our dreams of top shelf victory

be denied

As punishment she became locked up inside

Until she let herself out and cried

The dregs

You held my hand

as I walked out of my past

with the dregs clinging on

You held my hand

as I ventured into the present

and the dregs lost their hold

You hold my hand

as I look towards tomorrow

and smiling let the last dregs fall

away from me

For Idrissa Sané

My clothes get brighter
 as things get darker.
My hats are my disguise.
You may call it a mismatch
but I call it my tapestry
woven over the years.

Alex

Momentum is Everything

A hesitant start, a seed is sown
A slow step is taken into the unknown
its dark and unfriendly, but here we go
that's a glimmer of light on the horizon
over thorny bramble
digging in as we pass like barbed wire
wrapping itself around us using a
knife to set us free there are branches
and fallen trees to slow us down but, one
by one we carry on, climbing up and falling down
bruised knees, scratched ankles and hands
the stinging nettles have now attacked us
we are at a cross roads but which to take
I go left and you go right
I carry on with all my might, no longer
having to fight
This path is untrodden, head held high
I fake it to make it until it is true
Knowing that momentum is everything.

Perimeter

I stood on the perimeter as a silent onlooker

The tears were pouring down my face

all the negative feelings were overwhelming

Oh if my brain would obliterate these thoughts

they drew me into the centre, their affection

was contagious, a soft kiss was placed

upon my forehead and its ok not to be ok.

I just crumpled into a sobbing mess and held tight

My loyal friends stayed with me

And others said goodbye

Invisible Umbilical Cord

Going to bed was dreaded and horrible
where would the nightmare or dream take me
whilst nodding off my nerves in me
would wake me by jumping so high
again I would drift off going
out of my body looking down on myself
I'd soar off through the roof holding
tightly onto my silver threaded umbilical cord
which was all awhile attached to the
medically coshed body lying unmoving in
the bed. The cord was unleashed, bit by
bit like the moon to guide me across
the unknown night sky leading the way
to nightmarish encounters with the gremlin
from within, blowing the cobwebs of the
painful past away or showing a dream
of things to come.
As dawn approaches my silver cord
winds me backwards to where my body
lays once again I'm whole again
as I stir to awaken to a new day
to challenge my fears and taking small
steps to what might today bring
hope, love, joy and not fear, torment or sorrow
farewell till we meet again.

Musty Rug

She wasn't in a good place
Kneeling on the floor
Hands shaking as
She searched for keys to no avail
But took a shoe box out
Emptied it and placed some of the contents on the rug
She place the drawer back in the bureau
A memory box
The more she looked
Everything tipped all over the threadbare well loved rug
With missing tassels
She began to sob uncontrollably
With her face in the musty rug
"Oh what shall I do?"
She wailed knowing she couldn't leave this space without a key
To free her from the nightmare
She woke suddenly
Her face wet with tears
Wrapped in her own duvet
This was but a dream
She thought
I will sort out a drawer today
Make a memory box
To open up
For this was the key to her heart.

Musings of Donkeys

Oh what horrible conditions we lived in neglected and alone
Until finally eventually we got attention from a small women
dressed in soothing colours.
She went away.
We bowed our heads but to our glee she returned with a horse box
Could it be for me? And him?
We had no names our hooves were sore
Our nasty owner bridled us and pushed us unceremoniously
Until we were loaded on a mass of straw.
We were driven miles leaving our hell behind us.
We were unloaded gently and walked past a white house.
We saw the little woman through a window.
She was chopping something..
Could it be for us?
We were led to wonderful pastures to behold a stable all brand new.
Here she comes the little woman walking slowly but surely
To touch our matted heads so gently like a tickle.
Oh let's get to know her as she sits hour upon hour with us
in our home , our new home
We are no longer Eeyores just sometimes stubborn just for fun.
We have new names - I'm Oscar the cheeky one
who creeps up behind as she brushes Charlies grey coat
I sent the little woman flying once into the water butt -
no harm meant just jesting.
Once I picked up the hosepipe out of our bucket
and soaked the little woman.
And if she spends too much time with Charlie I butted her bum!
I can bray for her until she says "No"
and I breathe it out instead.
Poor Charlie cannot bray he only squeaks.
And now Charlie squeaks alone because I had to go.
I had to die.
And my little woman weeps into Charlies mane
And wishes to be butted once again.

My left shoulder

Jealousy created me bit by bit
In counselling I learnt that there was a pathway to help
To silence my inner gremlin who sits on my left shoulder
Dripping negative thoughts into my mind.
An angel of peace appeared and sat on my right shoulder
Negating the green eyed monster
So I can imagine myself lying in a field
meditating upon all the new inspiration I was given.

Hope Eternal

The little things that mean a lot
sometimes not recognised
for what they are.
Calming influences amongst a tempestuous sea, even forgotten.
Until they creep into your dreams and soothe you to sleep
slowly inhaling and exhaling letting go of the day
bit by bit from toe to head.
Beyond the mattress where you are sunk
tucked up tight and warm, head on the pillow.
You give yourself permission to drift off to dream your dream
until you wake refreshed
to take on the new day.

Everything is happening all at once

My brain is spinning like a wooden top
Oh slow down I tell myself
It's all a blur
Clouds and stars are flashing by
Too many to count
With fireballs lighting up the darkened sky
Suddenly day breaks with a narrow strip of colour
Creeping growing with silhouettes of tall Firs
And Beech trees revealing themselves to me.
I feel the warmth of the sun on my face
The smell of a warm waxed tent
This wakes me and frees my nightmares
A new day beckons
Do take care
Walk
Skip
Run
or just lie on the dewy grass.
These days of solitude recharge me
For I alone can decide what day this might be.

Spring birth and hope

As spring is sprung
budding flowers anew
the vivid greens of spring
bring hope of joyous dawn choruses
birth of lambs all jumping for joy
makes positive vibes of things to come
down this new park with a spring in your step
let's go forward, head up high
soaking up the warm Sundays
giving you thoughts so random and wild
you hope for your rebirth
that this path is tender and mild

Heartbreak

Splendid isolation leaves me cold
No contact with loved ones
Seeing them distancing
Makes my heart bleed.
Let's burst the bubble
And walk out with arms outstretched
Oh
For that cuddle.

I have my shadows

I have my shadows following me and
I don't know who they are
In the beginning there was a shaft of sunlight
In which danced tiny particles of dust
Where I saw the first light of day

She sat yawning pulling the covers off
She swung dangling her legs
Over the edge
And silently slid her feet onto the floor
Dust particles dancing around her
But surely
She had died long ago
Was this her strong spirit not letting go?

Advice from a Tree

I'd always watched you from afar
You always stopped and looked at me
The sadness a pain on your face
Wanted me to let my roots reach
Out to you and draw you to my
Strong unbending gnarly body
And wrap my branches around you
Reminding you that you too
Can stand strong and true
Unlike me you can move forward
Holding your head high letting
The sun shine on your face as
It shines through my leaves leaving
A dappled shadow on the
ground
Your shadow is always with
you
Changing like the seasons.

Please remember I am
Always with you.

Welcome to the next writer's section

Language of thought

written on skin

stories held long within, feel
the letters

caressing my arm

maybe you know how to read
this

language of skin

letters that sing

scribbles on skin

do you know
where to begin?

how to read
this
Braille
this
language

that demands to be felt

A hollow room

full of questions

and flickering light

emotion dancing

in empty spaces

I feel as though i am growing

even though

i am slowly dying

my mind changing its shape

time creeping up

so slowly

and silently

i

barely even notice it

at first

until

all of a sudden

the end

is right in

front

of

you

waiting

to change you

into

something else

Squaly change

pushing and pulling

hold steadfast

powerfully fragile

keep momentum

weary work

heavy heart and
aching mass

lie me among the dandelion grass

water me a while so

that i may bloom

The wisdom of becoming

the challenge of engaging

the complication of decision

LEAVING TO GROW

The wisdom of presence

the challenge of engaging

the complication of decision

THE WISDOM OF STAYING

The challenge of listening

The wisdom of decision

The complication of leaving

THE WISDOM OF GROWING

the complication of staying

Look how the lantern shines in the

crescent moon of night

wiping away old cobwebs and
cleaning the glass in the hope

that

you   might find

peace

within
the light
of a guiding star.

Home is where the heart is

but

where did I put mine?

i Have left it in so many places

pieces strewn across

the

world,

flitting around

like a hopeful caterpillar

to the places I feel safe

i thought at times

that I had lost my heart

put it somewhere so safe

that I was unable to find it

it turns out

it wasn't lost

just misplaced

and

now

this hopeful butterfly heart of mine

is preparing

to

soar

I hope that anyone
feeling alone
finds
some shelter
through
the sharing of some of my truths

Thank you
For being here
in a way that no else can
other than you.

Natasha k - w

"Dave"
David Robin Stretch

Alone

Being alone-
Most people say it with a sigh,
a downward glance, a lowered voice,
pity, even, for the person who
is alone.

You hear it all around.
Take Christmas.
Do you know someone,
maybe not young,
who will be alone
on Christmas Day?
They shouldn't be.
Invite them round
to join you and your family.
That may suit some,
great if they come
but please don't do that,
not to me.
Because, you see,
Alone is not the same as lonely.

But you'll be lonely.
No, I won't.
I'll simply be alone.
You must feel lonely.
No, I don't.
I'm happy being at home.

I spend a lot of time alone.
I'm my own usual company.
And that's ok, again I say,
Alone is not the same as lonely.

Dave Stretch

Enjoy This Day

Don't think of
all the things you should do,
just
enjoy this day

save yourself a big piece
of today
don't throw it away
enjoy this day

save yourself, I say
saving you will help save me
and her and him
and everyone you cannot see

we can't go out that much, can we?
By staying in, paradoxically
We are as one with everyone,
Working together, mutually
Part of a worldwide confederacy
Joined to more
than ever before.
Between ourselves,
in this day, we
have never ever
been so free.

So, I say,
Save yourself
a big piece of today
Don't throw it away,
Enjoy this day
Remember, it's not just for you-
For him and her and yes, me too.
Enjoy this day.

Dave Stretch

It takes time

It takes time to grow a toenail
And when you have then what?
You cut them, clip them, trim them down,
Then you start again
It takes time to grow a toenail

It's harvest time
Your crop is useless unless
A voodoo makes a doll of you
Then you won't be
growing toenails for yourself
zombie toenails, are they harvested
For more dolls, more zombies?
When will it end?

These days maybe we don't believe
In voodoo any more
Just geneticists who grow
Clones from DNA in nails
A copy of yourself
A clone from toenails
Cloenails
Beware chiropodists

Dave Stretch

Fields flat and flooded

Fields flat and flooded.
Sudden sheets of silver stain
the green grass

Grey ghostly gloom
fills the emptiness
between ground and sky.

Water seems to soak the air,
saturating space.
No light can sing its songs
in this dampened drear,
In this dank misery.

Sounds too subside
in a miasma of moist malevolence,
sinking into sodden thatch,
like rotting driftwood.

No edges to this state,
no way out, no escape,
no signs of a path to take.

And yet, accepting that's the case
does not mean being stuck in place.
As time goes by, weather will change,
Days will brighten, sun will heighten,
dry the fields, create a glow
sound will sharpen, grass will grow,
life will lighten.

All that's needed is time passing.
Endurance, love, will make it so.

Dave Stretch

Here, now.

I am content.
I chose to be here
and here I am.

I am satisfied, I guess.
Although it was effortless,
I have come here.

I am happy
because, you see,
I am with friends.

A sense of anticipation
at the thought of some creation.
An atmosphere of affirmation.
I feel safe.

Dave Stretch

Cuckoo

Oh, little birds, how foolish as to leave

your nest so unprotected, to receive

my egg, that you will hatch to grow for me

and I'll piss off. I won't be there to see

my offspring grow and bully yours

while you feed it until it soars.

It starves you as you really try

to help it launch into the sky.

I don't care what it drives you to.

I am Cuckoo. Fuck you.

Dave Stretch

Choices

When the worst thing happens,
that uproots the future,
I will resist.

It may well be
that I am powerless to
prevent it, in the end,
but I will try.

I will decide
if I want this,
if this new course
is the voyage I want to make.
I will decide that.

In the end, it may well be
that I make the journey
reluctantly.

I may decide that
Acceptance is preferable
To futile resistance
but that will be my choice.

Dave Stretch

Far and near

My last time in Kendal,

there were crowds,

at least by how it is today.

As I drew near,

they came to be

for some small time

a part of me enjoyed immersion.

I surfaced from them

by moving far,

and wallowed

in the peace of separation

Dave Stretch

Saturday Afternoon Rebirth

Chatter stumbles through the doorway
towing shopping bags and small
change,
ignoring football for the
hissing stir-fry of acquisition.

Other people's discarded memories
thrown into this Lilliputian skip of life
as entry to a beauty contest,
winners jigsaw pieces becoming
transplanted organs,
the frog in one person's eye,
the princess in another's,
ready to bloom a different flower, fresh life,
an untried fledgling in a new nest.

Scavengers suck the bones dry,
emptying the cauldron until
the coven of hyenas dissipates
leaving only gratitude,
a candle made from the residual wax
of past illuminations.

Then, unwanted scourings,
residue's residues,
are vacuumed up by
the vultures of last resort, the grim reapers of banalities,
to be digested into compost
for some unknown, unimagined garden.

New lives, rebirths.

Dave Stretch

Silence

Listen.
Just sit here in this quiet time and place and listen.
Listen.
Listen.
What you hear is silence. Our silence.
Listen.
Silence is the blank sheet of paper,
the canvas on which we will create together
So, listen.

Music.
Music is sounds placed in silence, both matter.
And you can hear our silence now.
It's beautiful.
We've created it.
We've started making music together
Without realising, with our silence.

Would you like to place a sound in it?
Any sound. Whatever you feel.
You can sing or hum, click, squeak, scream,
Clap your hands, drum the table,
Whisper. Blow raspberries, pop, breathe heavily, sigh.
Long or short, quiet or loud
that fits this silence.
When you make it, think beauty, not effect.
Do it. Place it. We'll listen.
Music!

Don't use too much of our silence-
Someone will answer you.
Allow them space.

Listeners, do you want to answer?
If they'd used words, you would.
So, make your sound, your answering sound.
Be beautiful, like them, for us, for all of us.
Aah.

Let's all join in, still listening
To others, to ourselves,
to the silence between the sounds.
Speak when it feels right,
if not, just listen, add to the silence.

Remember, when you make your sounds,
To listen, leave your ego.
Show something of yourself.
You may be loud, a dazzle of roses in full bloom.
But we're not all, some forget-me-nots.
Small and shy, still part of us.
It's our music, belongs to all of us

Let's take our place together,
Creating our own unique beauty
In this passing time and space.

Remember to listen.

Dave Stretch

space2create

Space2Create is a charity which aims to help people in our local community with physical and emotional difficulties. We use creative activity to support a pathway to wellbeing.

S2C Writers have worked together over the last 4 years and hope you enjoy some of our work in this first (ever!) anthology.

Unit 31
The Factory
Aynam Road
Kendal LA9 7DE

info@Space2Create.co.uk
www.Space2Create.co.uk
015394 82540

 find us on Facebook

 message us on Messenger

 Instagram
@space2createkendal